The Greatest Bible Stories Ever Told
The Good Shepherd

Stephen Elkins

AUTHOR

Tim O'Connor

ILLUSTRATIONS

BROADMAN & HOLMAN PUBLISHERS

NASHVILLE, TENNESSEE

THE WISE AND FOOLISH BUILDERS

Matthew 7:24 Everyone who hears these words of mine and puts them into practice is like a wise man who built his house upon the rock.

"Jesus said that everyone who hears the word of God and does what it says is like a wise man who built his house upon a rock. Our 'house' is our life and 'the rock' is God's Word! When we build our lives on the solid rock of God's Word, we will stand! When the rains of trouble come, we will stand! When the streams of sickness rise, we will stand! When the winds of change come and beat against our house, it will not fall down! Because it is built on the solid rock of God's Word!"

Now when Jesus finished His teaching, the crowd was amazed because He knew everything about the kingdom of God.

Affirmation: I will build my life on God's Word!

ONE LOST SHEEP

Luke 15:6b
Then he calls his friends and neighbors together and says, 'Rejoice with me; I have found my lost sheep.'

The church leaders in Jesus' day began to say bad things about Him because He invited tax collectors and sinners to eat with Him. So Jesus told this parable to show them that God loves everyone.

"What if you had a hundred sheep and one was lost? Wouldn't you leave the ninety-nine sheep in the meadow and look until you found the lost one?"

"And when you found him, wouldn't you be happy and carry the little lamb home on your shoulders? Then you'd call your friends together and say, 'Come celebrate with me for I have found my lost sheep!'

In the very same way, there is more celebration in heaven when one sinner comes to the Lord than over ninety-nine who do not need to repent. God is looking for lost sinners."

Affirmation: I will seek the lost!

THE PARABLE OF THE SOWER
Luke 8:11   This is the meaning of the parable: The seed is the word of God.

Once while a large crowd was gathering to see Jesus, He told this parable: "A farmer went out to plant his seeds. He took a handful and tossed them onto the ground."

"Some landed on the pathway to be stepped on and eaten by birds. Some landed upon the rocks, but before they could grow strong, they withered because their roots had no rich earth beneath them.

Other seeds fell among the thorns and were choked as they began to grow. But some of the seeds fell into the moist, rich earth and they grew healthy and strong. At harvest time, there were many crops; a hundred times more than the farmer sowed."

Then Jesus explained the meaning of the parable. "The seed is the Word of God. And like the seeds that fell along the pathway, some people hear the Word and receive it, but then the devil comes and confuses them and they no longer pay attention to God's Word. Because of this, they cannot be saved. And like the seeds that fell on the rocks, some people hear the Word of God and receive it with great joy. But then, when a time of trouble comes, they quickly fall away. This is because they have no deep roots of faith."

"The seeds that fall into the thorns are people who hear the Word of God and want to receive it, but their worries and cares of this life choke it out and they do not grow in faith.

But some seeds fall into the good soil and bear much fruit in God's kingdom. These are people who hear the Word of God. They memorize it, and work very hard to produce a good crop for the Lord."

Affirmation: I will bear much fruit in God's kingdom!

9

ASK, SEEK, AND KNOCK

Matthew 7:7 Ask and it will be given to you; seek and you will find; knock and the door will be opened to you.

Matthew writes concerning prayer, "Sometimes it takes a little time for prayers to be answered. But Jesus taught the people that they should never stop praying. Keep asking in prayer, and it will be given to you; keep seeking, and you will find what you are looking for; keep knocking, and the door will be opened for you! For God always hears our prayers. And He will answer; sometimes yes, sometimes no, sometimes wait."

"If you were a father and your child asked for bread, would you give him a stone? Or if your child asked for a fish, would you give him a snake? If we know how to give good gifts to our children, think of how much our Heavenly Father will give good gifts to those that ask Him! Treat others like you would want them to treat you: this is the golden rule!"

Affirmation: I will treat others like I would like them to treat me!

11

THE LORD'S PRAYER

Matthew 6:9 Our Father which art in heaven,
Hallowed be thy name.

Matthew was a disciple of Jesus. As they traveled together, he would write down what Jesus taught. Matthew writes: "Jesus said that there is a right way to pray and a wrong way to pray. We should not say our prayers in front of people just to make them think we're good. This is a wrong reason to pray.

When we pray, we should go into our room, close the door, and pray to our heavenly Father in secret. God promises to answer this kind of prayer by rewarding us openly. Jesus said, when you pray, use this example:

*Our Father, which art in heaven
Hallowed be Thy name. Thy kingdom come,
Thy will be done*

*on earth as it is in heaven.
Give us this day our daily bread.
Forgive us our debts as we forgive
our debtors. And lead us not
into temptation, but deliver
us from evil. For Thine is the
kingdom, the power and the
glory forever and ever."*

JOURNEY to the CROSS

The feast of the Passover was only a few short days away.
Jesus called His disciples together and said, "We are going
to Jerusalem. There, all the things written about Me by the
prophets will happen. I will be handed over to Roman
leaders. I will be unkindly treated, and there I will die. But
three days later I will come back to life again."

A HOUSE OF PRAYER

Luke 19:46 *"It is written," **he said to them,** "'My house will be a house of prayer'; but you have made it 'a den of robbers.'"*

On Monday, Jesus entered the temple in Jerusalem. He became very angry at the money changers and those buying and selling doves in God's house. He overturned their tables and drove them all out of the temple. Then He began to teach, "Is it not written, 'My house shall be called a house of prayer?' You have made it a robber's house!" When the priests heard what Jesus had done, they wanted rid of Him.

On Tuesday, Jesus awoke and returned to Jerusalem. Once again, He was greeted by huge crowds who followed Him everywhere. The religious leaders began to worry. "What if Jesus leads the people against us? We could lose our power. We must stop Him!" They said, "Let's trick Jesus into saying something bad about Rome. Then Rome will arrest Him, and we'll be done with Him!"

Affirmation: I will follow Jesus too!

THIRTY PIECES OF SILVER

Luke 22:5 They were delighted and agreed to give him money.

That night Judas Iscariot, one of the twelve disciples, went to see the church leaders. "I know that you want Jesus removed," he said. "What will you give me if I help you?" They counted out thirty pieces of silver. Judas agreed and started planning to betray Jesus.

Affirmation: I will be faithful to Jesus!

THE UPPER ROOM

Luke 22:12 *"He will show you a large upper room, all furnished. Make preparations there."*

On Thursday evening, Jesus and His twelve disciples met in an upper room to celebrate the Passover. The meal was prepared by Peter and John. He taught them many things that evening. He said that being "the greatest" meant that we must serve others. Then He washed their feet as an example of what a servant does. When it came time to eat, Jesus took some bread, blessed it, and gave it to His disciples saying, "Take this bread and eat it; for it is My body." And they all ate.

Then taking the cup, He gave thanks and said, "This is My blood, which is spilled out for many. Do this in remembrance of Me." And they all drank. This was the first communion service.

As the mealtime ended, Jesus spoke once more. "Tonight, I am giving you a new commandment. Love one another. If you do this, everyone will know you are My disciples." They sang a song and together they went back to the Mount of Olives.

PRAYER IN THE GARDEN

Luke 22:39 *Jesus went out as usual to the Mount of Olives, and his disciples followed him.*

Now there was a beautiful garden near the Mount of Olives called Gethsemane. Jesus and His disciples went there late Thursday night. Jesus said to them, "Sit here while I go and pray." He took Peter, James, and John with Him.

"My heart is about to break with sorrow," **Jesus told them.** "Please stay awake and keep watch for Me." Then Jesus walked a little further and fell to the ground praying.

"Father, if it is possible, let these terrible things which are about to happen go away. Yet I am willing to do what You want, not what I want."

And Jesus prayed so very hard that the sweat on His forehead became drops of blood falling to the ground.

When He returned to His disciples, He found them all asleep. Jesus returned to pray a second and third time. But each time He found his disciples sleeping. Then Jesus knew the worst was about to happen. "Look," He said, "My betrayer is coming!"

Affirmation: I want to do God's will!

18

THE BETRAYER COMES

Luke 22:54a   Then siezing him, they led him away and took him into the house of the high priest.

Through the darkness and down the narrow pathway came a mob of people carrying torches and clubs. Following was a small group of Roman soldiers. Judas was leading the way. He had told the mob to grab the one he would kiss and to take Him away. With the mob behind him, Judas stood face to face with Jesus.
"Master," said Judas. Then he kissed Jesus. The mob grabbed Him.

Peter pulled out his sword. While trying to protect Jesus, he swung and cut off the ear of one of the chief priest's guards.

"Put away the sword!" shouted Jesus. Then Jesus reached out, touched, and healed the servant's ear. There in the darkness the Roman soldiers and the Jewish leaders bound Jesus and took Him away. The disciples were afraid and fled into the night.

Affirmation: With Jesus I am not afraid!

19

THE TRIALS OF JESUS

Luke 23:4   *Then Pilate announced to the chief priests and the crowd, "I find no basis for a charge against this man."*

Early Friday morning the many trials of Jesus began. People lied to judges about things Jesus had said and done. He was spat upon, beaten, and terribly abused.

When Judas saw what was happening to Jesus, he was filled with sorrow. He knew he had sinned. He went to the temple and begged them to release Jesus, but they would not listen. Judas threw his coins on the temple floor and ran away. He could no longer live with himself knowing what he had done to Jesus.

Finally, Jesus was brought before Pontius Pilate, the Roman governor and judge. The Jewish leaders kept saying things that were untrue. "He says He's a king. And He says we should not pay taxes to Caesar!" Pilate looked at Jesus, who had been badly beaten, and asked, "Are You the King of the Jews?" Jesus replied, "My kingdom is not in this world."

"Then You are a king?" asked Pilate again. "You say correctly that I am a king," answered Jesus. "But I come to this world to tell people the truth."

"What is truth?" asked Pilate. Then he said, "I find no wrong in this man. Let Him go."

Each year during the Passover celebration the Roman governor would release one prisoner. The people would decide which one. Pilate knew that the Jewish leaders were accusing Jesus because they were jealous of Him. "The people love Jesus," he thought. "So I'll let them choose between Jesus and that terrible murderer named Barabbas. Surely the people will choose Jesus!"

So Pilate spoke to the crowd that had gathered. "Should Jesus be set free, or Barabbas?" To Pilate's surprise, he heard them shouting "Barabbas! Free Barabbas!"

"What shall I do with Jesus?" Pilate asked the crowd. "Kill Him! Crucify Him!" they shouted. Louder and louder their cries rang out until Pilate, fearing a riot, decided to please them.

Affirmation: I will choose Jesus to be my savior!

THE CRUCIFIXION

Luke 24:6 He has risen!

Jesus was then turned over to the Roman soldiers. They stripped off His clothes and beat Him with a whip. They made fun of Him by putting a purple robe on His back and placing a crown of thorns on His head.

Jesus was silent. Then they put His own clothes back on Him and led Him away to a place called Golgotha to be crucificied.

On Friday morning they crucified Jesus and two lawbreakers, one on the right and the other on the left. As Jesus hung on the cross He was heard to say, "Father forgive them, for they do not know what they are doing."

Then one of the lawbreakers hanging with Jesus said, "If you really are the King of the Jews, save Yourself!" But the other lawbreaker said, "Be quiet! We deserve to die because we have done so many bad things. This man has done nothing wrong. Jesus, Jesus, remember me."

Jesus looked at this man and said, "Today you will be with Me in heaven." A great darkness fell over the land for three hours. Jesus cried out from the cross with a loud voice, "It is finished! Father, I give to You My Spirit." And having said this, He died.

Jesus' body was placed in the borrowed tomb of a secret disciple named Joseph. They rolled a large stone in front of the opening and went away.

On Sunday morning, a woman named Mary Magdalene and the other Mary came to the tomb. They found the giant stone had been rolled away. Upon the stone sat an angel who said, "Jesus is not here. He is alive! Quickly now, go tell His disciples."

They ran like the wind to tell the disciples. "Jesus has risen! He's alive!" They were so happy!

Jesus appeared to many people. He walked with two followers on the Emmaus Road. Then Jesus visited the disciples in Jerusalem as they gathered to eat supper. "Peace be with you," Jesus said. He ate with them and showed them His nail-scarred hands and feet.

Jesus was truly alive ... He had risen from the grave!
"Remember what I said on the way to Jerusalem several
days ago? 'I will be handed over to the Roman leaders. I
will be unkindly treated and, just like the prophets said, I
will die and on the third day I will come back to life again.'
All these things you have now seen."

"Now you must go into every nation and tell them the good news of God's coming kingdom. Tell them that if they believe in Me and My words, they will live forever, just like Me!"

Jesus stayed with the disciples awhile longer. Then after He had blessed each of them, He said, "I am going now to live with My Father and your Father. Be sure that I am always going to be with you."

Then Jesus rose up into the air until He disappeared in the clouds.

As they were gazing into the sky, two men in white clothing stood beside them and said, "One day Jesus will come again in this very same way." Then the disciples returned to Jerusalem to start their ministries.

Affirmation: I believe Jesus died and rose again for me!

THE LAMB'S BOOK OF LIFE

Revelation 21:27 Nothing impure will ever enter it, nor will anyone who does what is shameful or deceitful, but only those whose names are written in the Lamb's book of life.

It's wonderful to know that we serve a living Savior. He is at this very moment preparing our homes in heaven. And one day soon, Jesus will break through the clouds and come back to this earth to claim His children. Satan, that old serpent, will be defeated. Then comes the greatest moment in history when Jesus opens the "Lamb's Book of Life."

If you have asked Jesus to come into your heart, your name will be written in the Lamb's Book of Life. Just think ... God knows your name, and has heard your prayers. If you've never asked Jesus into your heart, but you want to, just pray this little prayer:

Dear Heavenly Father, I believe that Jesus died on a cross for me, and I believe He rose again and lives today. Please forgive me of all my sins and let Jesus come into my heart. Amen.

COLLECT ALL 10

Word & Song AUDIO BOOK

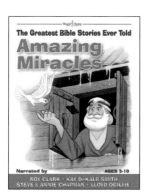

The Greatest Bible Stories Ever Told
Amazing Miracles
Narrated by
ROY CLARK • KAY DeKALB SMITH
STEVE & ANNIE CHAPMAN • LLOYD OGILVIE
AGES 3-10

0-8054-2471-7

The Greatest Bible Stories Ever Told
God's Power
Narrated by
LLOYD OGILVIE • DEAN STONE
GEORGE BEVERLY SHEA
AGES 3-10

0-8054-2466-0

The Greatest Bible Stories Ever Told
Stories of Faith
Narrated by
LARNELLE HARRIS
STEVE & ANNIE CHAPMAN • LLOYD OGILVIE
AGES 3-10

0-8054-2470-9

The Greatest Bible Stories Ever Told
Stories that **Build Character**
Narrated by
LARNELLE HARRIS • STEVE GREEN
LLOYD OGILVIE
AGES 3-10

0-8054-2469-5

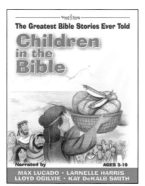

The Greatest Bible Stories Ever Told
Children in the Bible
Narrated by
MAX LUCADO • LARNELLE HARRIS
LLOYD OGILVIE • KAY DeKALB SMITH
AGES 3-10

0-8054-2474-1

The Greatest Bible Stories Ever Told
Courage & Strength
Narrated by
REGGIE WHITE • LARNELLE HARRIS
STEVE GREEN • LLOYD OGILVIE • STEVE CAMP
AGES 3-10

0-8054-2468-7

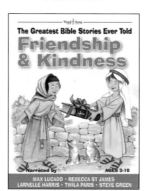

The Greatest Bible Stories Ever Told
Friendship & Kindness
Narrated by
MAX LUCADO • REBECCA ST JAMES
LARNELLE HARRIS • TWILA PARIS • STEVE GREEN
AGES 3-10

0-8054-2473-3

The Greatest Bible Stories Ever Told
The Good Shepherd
Narrated by
STEVE GREEN
JERRY FALWELL • ANNIE CHAPMAN
AGES 3-10

0-8054-2475-x

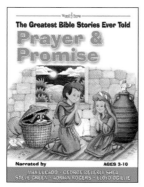

The Greatest Bible Stories Ever Told
Prayer & Promise
Narrated by
MAX LUCADO • GEORGE BEVERLY SHEA
STEVE GREEN • ADRIAN ROGERS • LLOYD OGILVIE
AGES 3-10

0-8054-2472-5

Available in Your Favorite Christian Bookstore.

The Greatest Bible Stories Ever Told
Special Families
Narrated by
JONI EARECKSON TADA • TWILA PARIS • STEVE GREEN
LLOYD OGILVIE • STEVE & ANNIE CHAPMAN
AGES 3-10

0-8054-2467-9

We hope you enjoyed this Word & Song Storybook.